📖 Need to Read SERIES

Think
Like a Winner

DR. NORMAN VINCENT PEALE

Tyndale House Publishers, Inc.
WHEATON, ILLINOIS

Front cover photo: Bob Taylor Photography

Unless otherwise noted, Scripture quotations are from *The
Simplified Living Bible,* copyright © 1990 by KNT
Charitable Trust. All rights reserved. Quotations marked
NIV are from the *Holy Bible,* New International Version.
Copyright © 1973, 1978, 1984 International Bible
Society. Used by permission of Zondervan Bible Publishers.

Adapted for the Need to Read Series from *Six Attitudes for
Winners* by Dr. Norman Vincent Peale, Tyndale House
Publishers, Pocket Guides. Copyright © 1987 by Norman
Vincent Peale.

ISBN 0-8423-7085-4
Library of Congress Catalog Card Number 90-71456
Copyright © 1990 by Tyndale House Publishers, Inc.
All rights reserved
Printed in the United States of America

96 95 94 93
9   8   7   6   5   4   3   2

CONTENTS

CHAPTER 1
Being a "Yes" Person

Once I was talking with J.C. Penney. You may know his name from the chain of stores he started. But J.C. had been a friend of mine for a long time. Now he was ninety-five years old, but still sharp. We started talking about problems.

"You have had many problems in your long life," I said. "How do you deal with them?"

His answer was wise. "Well, Norman," he said, "I am glad for my problems. I dealt with each problem as it came along. Each time, I got a little stronger. That helped me deal with the next problem."

What was J.C. Penney's secret? He said yes to life. He even said yes to his problems.

So how can you deal with your problems? Just say yes.

Facts
Sometimes facts can be hard. Some people look at a fact and say, "That's the way it is. There's nothing I can do about it. A fact is a fact. You just can't get

around it." The person who talks like that is a "No" Person.

The Yes Person looks at it in a new way. "Yes, here is a fact. But there is a way to deal with it. Go around it. Go under it. Go over it. Or hit it straight on. A problem is for solving. And that's what I'm going to do."

I have a sign in my office. A friend made it for me. It says, "The way you think counts more than the facts." That saying helps me handle my problems. The No Person is always thinking no. He sees the facts and gives up. The Yes Person sees the same facts. But he thinks about them in a new way. In this way, the Yes Person wins over his problems.

Two Salesmen

There were two salesmen. They both got jobs in a tough city. The city was "tough" because the people just did not buy things. Other salesmen were glad to be sent to other places. "No one can sell a thing in that city," they said.

The first salesman knew this. He knew his chances were not good. It would be hard to sell things. He did not think he would do very well there. "So," he said, "why knock myself out? It's just not fair for them to put me in this tough city. There's no way I can win here."

Guess what happened. He failed, of course. He did not sell a thing. Then he quit. He never really tried.

The second salesman was new to this work. He did

not know how tough the city was. He just knew that there were lots of people there. *People need my product,* he thought. *And I am here to sell it to them.*

He worked hard. And guess what? He sold a lot. He was a great success.

If someone said, "This is a really tough city," he would have laughed. "No way!" he would say. "Maybe I have to work a little harder. But that doesn't mean I can't sell here."

He was a Yes Person. He thought he could win, and he did. The first salesman was a No Person. His own thinking made him fail.

Three Steps

How can you become a Yes Person? There are three steps.

1. *Think, don't react.* When hard times hit, some people react. They get upset. They panic. Maybe they start to hate the person who brought the hard times. But most of the time, these ways are not the best.

You must train yourself to keep calm. Think through the matter. Cool it. Our minds do not work best when they are hot. But cool minds think up smart answers.

2. *Look for the "how."* My friend Fred owned his own firm. Things went well until his partner started cheating. Fred lost it all.

But instead of feeling bad, he started over. He started a new firm. Once again, he was a success. He told me, "I decided I would not be an 'if' thinker, but a 'how' thinker."

The "if" thinker keeps saying, "If only I had done this. If only this had happened." He keeps looking back. He never gets ahead.

The "how" thinker is always looking for the answer. If he has a problem, he knows there is a way to solve it. He looks for that way. "How can I use this problem to help me?" he asks. "How can I get something good out of it?"

3. *Believe that you can.* If you tell yourself that you can't, you won't. But if you tell yourself you can, it helps you try harder. That extra effort makes things happen.

The Bible talks a lot about faith. Here is one great verse. "The Holy Spirit doesn't want you to be afraid of people. He wants you to be wise and strong, and to love them" (2 Timothy 1:7). We should stop thinking about what we can't do. That's the spirit of fear. We should start thinking about what God can do through us.

Buried Treasure

When I was young, I went to see an older friend. I needed his advice. He always seemed to know what to say.

"I have a problem," I said.

"Great!" he answered.

That seemed like a strange answer to me. "Great?" I asked. "What's so great about it?"

He smiled. Then he spoke. "Out of this problem, some great new thing may come into your life."

He asked me to tell him about my problem. I gave him all the details.

"There it is," he said in his wise way. "This big problem of yours." He acted as if my problem was sitting on the table. Just a big blob in front of us. "Don't be afraid of it," he said. "It doesn't look so mean. It is really smiling at you. It wants to play hide-and-seek with you. There is something great hidden inside of it. It will be fun for you to find it."

He poked his finger at the make-believe blob. "Every problem has a soft spot," he said. "We'll find it."

As we talked, I did find it. From that problem I learned one of the greatest lessons of my life. Since then I have treated my problems with more respect. Each one has some gift inside. Each one has some treasure to give me.

So don't fight a problem. And don't complain. Instead, start asking questions. See what you can learn from your problems. See what God is trying to teach you.

Cutting It Down to Size

Problems seem much bigger than we are. They seem so big that they scare us. But they aren't that big, really. We tend to blow them up in our minds. We make them bigger than they really are.

We must see each problem as it really is. We must cut it down to size. If we see how small it is, we won't be so scared.

Once I saw a man in an office doing something strange. He had sheets of paper on the desk in front of him. Each sheet had something written on it. They were neatly lined up on the desk.

"You may wonder what I'm doing," he said. (He was right!) "I am dealing with a pretty rough problem. This is how I do that."

He went on to tell his story. At one time he was "licked" by his problems. Then a man told him, "Divide them up. Look, no problem is as big as it seems. If you take it apart, you can deal with each part. Take a problem in bits and pieces. Then it won't look so big."

"That advice made sense," my friend told me. "So now I do this. I write down the parts of the problem. Each part is on a new page. Then I pray and ask God to help me."

"Most of the time," he went on, "I deal with the easy parts first. Then I pray again. Then I deal with another part. One at a time, I deal with them all."

He seemed very happy as he told me this. "You know," he said, "I feel great now. I'm getting a real kick out of life. I know I am bigger than any problem."

God's Phone Number

You can beat any problem. But not always by yourself. You need God's help. And he is ready to give it. You and God are a team. Could any problem be too big for that team?

One woman told me about her problems. She had been very sick as a child. Now she was crippled. But she seemed very happy in spite of all this.

"What's your secret?" I asked her.

"Oh," she smiled. "I have God's phone number. I can call him any time. And the line is never busy. He always answers."

"What is God's phone number?" I asked.

"It's JER 33:3. That is, the book of Jeremiah, chapter 33, verse 3. It says, 'Call to me and I will answer you. I will show you great and mighty things'" (NIV).

Now you have God's phone number, too. Now you can handle your problems. All you have to do is call. He is waiting to hear from you. He will answer you right away. He can show you a way out of your problems. He can help you win over them.

CHAPTER 2

Facing Your Fears

> "The first thing a man should do is to get rid of fear. . . . A man is a slave until he gets fear under his feet." — Thomas Carlyle

You can get rid of fear.

This simple thought is one of the first steps. If you want to get rid of your fear, start here. Start with the thought, *I can get rid of fear.* Do not think that you have to live with fear all your life.

Facing Life's Storms

An old cowboy once said he had learned a lesson from cows. In the winter, bad storms can kill cows. Out on the ranch, the freezing rain and ice come down hard. The wind piles the snow into large drifts.

Most cows turn away from the wind. They let the wind drive them across the land. They stop when they reach a fence. The cows just pile up there. The snow blows over them. The cows are buried in the drifts.

But one kind of cow does not do this. The Hereford cows face into the wind. They stand there, shoulder to shoulder, and put their heads down. The wind blows over them. It blows against them. But it does not move them.

"Almost always, you find the Herefords alive and well," this cowboy says. "That is the best lesson I ever learned. Face life's storms."

This lesson is good. Do not run away from your fears. Decide to face them. When someone stands up to something, that something tends to fold. It is far better to face your fears head-on.

Besides, most fears are silly and empty. A friend of mine figured something out about his own fears. He said that 92 percent of the things he feared never happened. Only 8 percent of these things did happen. And how did he handle these? "Oh," he says, "I just stood up to them. I handled them and won over them."

End Your Fear of People

In my younger years, I worked as a newsman in Detroit. My boss at the paper was wise and kind. Once he called me into his office to give me some advice.

"Norman," he said, "you seem very fearful. You must get rid of this fear. What in the world is there to be afraid of? Why should you go through life like a scared rabbit? The good Lord has told us that he would help us. He will take care of us."

TWO FAITH THOUGHTS

- Psalm 34:4: "I cried to him and he answered me! He freed me from all my fears."
- Psalm 23:4: "I will fear no evil, for you are with me" (NIV).

If you always know that God is with you, fear will fade away.

That talk will always stay in my mind. "Look, son," he went on, "I'm going to give you some advice. The only one in this world to fear is God. And that doesn't mean to be afraid of him. It means to give him honor and respect. There is nothing else to fear. There is no one else you need to be afraid of."

"But, sir," I said, "that's a pretty big order. How can I go through my whole life without fear?"

He looked at me and waved his finger. It was dark with printer's ink. "Listen," he said, "I'll tell you. The answer is in the Bible. Joshua 1:9 says to be strong and brave. Do not be afraid. For the Lord your God is with you in any place you go. Just hang on to that promise."

"And don't forget," he added, "who made that promise. It's Someone who never lets you down."

The world is full of sad, fearful people. Why are

they sad? Their fear keeps them from having friends.
At least it gets in the way of good friendships. The
worker fears his boss. The quiet person fears people
who talk a lot. Wives are afraid of their husbands.
Husbands are afraid of their wives. Some parents are
even afraid of their kids.

In many cases, fearful people stay away from things.
They don't want to get involved when other people do
something. There might be someone there who scares
them.

ADVICE FROM STONEWALL

Stonewall Jackson was a leader in the South during
the Civil War. One night he was meeting with the
other leaders of his army. They were planning a
daring attack. The odds were against them. But they
had a chance to win big.

After the meeting, one of the other leaders came
up to Jackson. "But, sir," he said, "I'm afraid of
this plan. I'm afraid we can't quite carry it off."

As the story goes, Jackson stood up. He put his
hand on the man's shoulder. "Never take the
advice of your fears," he said. "Never take the
advice of your fears."

How can you get over this fear of other people?

1. *Help other shy people.* In any group, there are other shy people. Find a person like this and talk with him or her. It will help you both. You might also find another kind of shyness. Some people who talk a lot are really afraid. They think people don't like them. So they are trying too hard to fit in. Under all the words, there is often a shy person who needs a friend.

2. *Be yourself.* There is only one of you. You are special. This means you don't have to copy others. You can be who you really are. When you try to copy others, you are showing fear. You are trying to be the other person. Why? Because you think people won't like the real you. Don't do this. Tell yourself how special you are.

3. *Love others.* The Bible says, "Perfect love drives out fear" (1 John 4:18, NIV). Learn to love others — really love them. Talk with them. Ask about their lives. Do kind things for them. This will help you build normal friendships. There will be no place for fear.

4. *Pray for people you are afraid of.* Ask God to help them with their problems. (They have problems too, you know.) In time, they will sense your care for them. They may return it.

LOVE BEATS FEAR

A young man told me he was afraid of his boss. The boss was mean. He frowned all the time. No one got close to him.

"I almost shake when I am called to his office," the young man said. "But I have to report to him every day."

I said that the boss might be lonely. Or he might be facing some trouble. Maybe that would explain why he was so mean. I told the man to pray for his boss. He should try to be friendly to him, I said. "It will be like trying to dent a wall of steel," the man said.

But it did not turn out that way. As the young man prayed for his boss, things changed. He was kind to his boss each day. His fears faded away. The boss became friendly to him.

This is how it often works. Real love melts away the fear of other people.

To break free from your fear of other people, try this. Become aware of their needs. Get your mind off yourself. Think about what you can do for the person you fear.

CHAPTER 3

End Your Fear of Failure

Many people are afraid of failing. This hurts them deeply. You see, people "freeze up" when they have this fear. And that often makes them fail. So the fear of failure often leads to failure. (And that can lead to more fear.)

All of us fail. At one time or other, we all lose. The question is, How do you react?

Failure can teach us many things. We can learn from our mistakes. We can also learn from our successes. We should be looking for lessons in both our wins and losses. We should look for new thoughts. We should build our know-how. In this way, we can turn failure into success.

> "No one is as old as the person who stops having fun." — Henry David Thoreau

So what should you do when you fail? First, look at what happened. Look at all the details. Then, ask yourself, "Why did I fail?"

Once you know why you failed, you can change

things. You will be wiser. You will know what not to do. And you can try again.

Do not ever think that you will always fail. Think about the success that will come from your new wisdom.

It is great to win over this fear of failing. It sets you free to try new things. In order to win, you need to plan. You need to learn. You need to think. You need to study. You need to work. You need to believe. And you need to pray. Then you will have all you need to beat this fear.

How to Be Brave

How can you be brave? What's the secret? *Be honest.* Admit your feelings of failure. Admit your fears. Then ask for God's help and go on. Do your job in spite of these feelings and fears.

Have you ever heard of Maurice Chevalier (SHEV-all-YAY)? This French singer was the greatest of his time. But in the middle of his career, something strange happened. One night, before going on stage, he felt dizzy. His brain felt like it was on fire. He heard the lines of the other actors, but they seemed far away. He tried to get back on track. But his mind was a jumble. He felt lost.

His fellow actors tried to cover up for him that night. But this went on for weeks. He had lost his special flair. He was known for his grace. He was famous for the easy way he sang and spoke. Now he would stop and start and stutter. For the first time in his life, he was failing.

He told his doctor, "I'm a beaten man. I'm afraid of being a failure. There is no future for me now."

The doctor ordered him to rest. The singer moved to southern France. He was to take long walks and relax. This would calm his nerves. But the inner fears stayed with him. He had lost all his grace. He was not sure of anything. He was afraid, very afraid.

The doctor then said he should sing at the town hall. There was a show there with a small crowd. They would love to hear him sing.

"But," said Maurice, "how can I do this? This scares me to death. How can I be sure my mind won't go blank?"

"You can't be sure," the doctor said. "But you must not be afraid of failing. You are afraid to step out on stage. So you keep telling yourself you can't. You say that you have no future. But fear is never a reason for quitting. It is only an excuse. When a brave man fights his fear, he admits that he is afraid. Then he goes on in spite of it."

Maurice was very afraid. Even in front of that small crowd, he was scared. But he went on stage. He sang very well. He felt joy inside. "I knew that the fear was still there," he said later. "All I did was admit my fear and go on. It worked."

As the years went by, Maurice sang again and again.

He became famous again. "There have been many times of fear," he said. "The doctor was right. I can never be sure I won't fail. But fear is no reason to quit.

"If you wait for the perfect moment," he added, "it won't come. Don't wait to be sure of success, because you never will be. If you want to be safe, you will wait and wait. You will not climb mountains. You will not win races. You will not become truly happy."

So don't be afraid to be afraid. Be honest. Admit your fear. But then act as if you were not afraid. With the help of God, go on. Do your job. Don't let fear stop you.

CHAPTER 4
Life Is Fun

You can tell when people are having fun in life. They
show joy in all that they do. They are fun to be with.
They seem to be able to do new things.

I am talking about a special kind of fun. It is not just
telling jokes. It is not laughing at others. It is joy. It
comes when life excites you.

This kind of fun is a lot like faith. It is faith on fire.
It is a great gift from God.

Do you know any children? What is so special about
them? They have fun. A little child is in love with life.
He thinks the world is great. Each new bit of life gives
him something to play with.

One writer said that this was the secret of genius. You
have to carry the spirit of a child into your old age. Never
lose that sense of fun. Never lose that desire to play.

But most people do lose that sense of fun. They do
lose their desire to play. As they grow older, it just
goes down the drain.

Maybe you are like that. Life does not excite you
very much. Well, let's take a good look at fun. Let's
see if we can get more fun out of life.

Seeing with New Eyes

My mother had a lot of joy. She had great fun with even the normal things of life. She saw romance and glory in all that happened.

One night stays in my mind. It was foggy. We were on a ferry boat from New Jersey to New York. I found no fun there. There was so much fog, I could not see. But my mother said, "Isn't this thrilling?"

"What is thrilling?" I asked.

"Why," she said, "the fog is. The lights are. See the other ferry boat that went by? Look at its lights. They are fading away into the mist. It is all so thrilling!"

Just then, we heard a fog horn. It sounded deep and full. My mother's face lit up. She was having fun with all of this. I just wanted to get to the other side.

She stood at the rail of the boat. She looked at me. I knew she was about to say something. "Norman," she said softly. "I have been giving you advice all your life. Some you have taken. Some you have not taken. But here is some advice you have to take. Make up your mind right now that the world is fun. It is thrilling, Norman. It is full of beauty. Never forget that. Love the world. Love its beauty. Love its people."

It is simple advice. But it leads to a life full of joy.

Little Miss No One

One night I met "Miss No One." I was visiting a city on the West Coast. I had just given a speech. A young woman came up to me. She spoke to me in a very quiet voice.

"I just wanted to shake hands with you," she said. "But I really shouldn't bother you. There are so many great people here. I'm no one."

She was about to leave, but I stopped her. "Please stay," I said. "I'd like to talk with you."

After saying hello to a few others, I turned to her again. "Now, Miss No One, let's talk."

"What did you call me?" she asked.

"I called you by your name," I answered. "At least that's the only name you gave me. You told me you were No One. Do you have some other name?"

"Of course," she said. "You see, I don't feel very good about myself. That's why I came tonight. I was hoping you would say something to help me."

"Well," I said, "I'm saying it now. You are a child of God." I told her to say that each day. She should stand up tall and repeat those words. "I am a child of God." I went on to tell her other things. I'm saying some of the same things in this book. I told her how to enjoy life. I told her how to feel better about herself.

Not long ago, I was back in the same area. A pretty young woman came up to me. "Don't you know who I am?" she teased. "I'm Miss No One. Well, I used to be Miss No One." She had a big smile. There was a sparkle in her eyes. She had changed a great deal.

This proves a simple fact. You can change! Any

person can change! Even if you are a dull "no one," you can change. You can become a happy "someone."

How to Do It

1. *Start the day right.* The first five minutes of a day mean a lot. What are you telling yourself in those five minutes? One great man used to lie in bed and think. He would think of all the good news he knew. Then he got up in a great mood. He went out to a world full of good things.

Another man says this. "Each morning, pull yourself up to your full height. Stand tall. Then think tall. Think great thoughts. Then go out and act tall. If you do that, joy will flow to you."

If you spread that joy through the day, you will have joy yourself.

2. *Read your Bible.* It is full of things to perk you up. Can you think of any better saying than this? "I can do everything God asks me to with the help of Christ" (Philippians 4:13).

The Bible just glows with fun and joy. "Be made new," it says, "in the attitude of your minds" (Ephesians 4:23, NIV). Not merely in the top level of your mind. But in your deep spirit. That's where you need to become new. If you keep reading the Bible, that will happen. Then pray to God and get going!

Here's an idea. Each morning, before you start the

day, say this. "This is the day the Lord has made. I will rejoice and be glad in it" (Psalm 118:24). Say that three times. Then get up and start the day.

3. *Love life and people.* Love the sky. Love beauty. Love God. The person who loves has fun in life. Begin today. That's right. Start working on this love for life.

You could be like Fred, for example. Fred runs a little eating place. I stopped in there once.

He put his big hand down on the counter. "OK, brother," he said, "What will you have?"

"Are you Fred?" I asked. After all, it *was* "Fred's Diner."

"Yes," he answered.

"They tell me you make good burgers," I said.

"Brother," he said smiling, "you never ate such burgers!"

"OK," I said, "let me have one."

There was one other man sitting at the counter. He was an old man and he looked sad. He was hunched over. His hand was shaking.

Fred gave me my burger. Then he moved down to this man. He touched the man's hand. "That's all right, Bill," he said. "That's all right. I'm going to fix you a bowl of hot soup. You'd like that, right?" The man nodded.

Then a man got up from a booth. He paid the check and headed outside. "Mr. Brown," Fred said, "be careful. Watch out for those cars out there. They come by pretty fast at night." Then he added, "And take a look at the moon. See how it shines on the river. It's very pretty tonight."

When I paid my check, I just had to say something. "You know something, Fred? I like the way you spoke to those old men. You made them feel that life is good."

"Why not?" he asked. "Life *is* good. Me, I get a kick out of living. Those two are pretty sad old guys. This place is sort of like home to them. And I kind of like them, too."

Find needs and fill them. Look for what other people need. Then meet those needs. That will bring fun and joy to your life.

"The poorest person is the one who has lost the thrill of life. Let a man lose it all. But let him keep the thrill of life. He will come back again to success." — H.W. Arnold

---

4. *Keep your power up.* When you are tense, you lose power. It takes so much out of you. You worry about this. You worry about that. That's hard work! You get tired when you worry like that!

Learn to "let go and let God." Let go of your own worries. Let God take care of them. Ask God to guide you through life. Then you will have the power to live life fully. Then you will be able to enjoy it.

CHAPTER 5

Break Free from Worry

Worry can wreck your body. It may be all in your mind. But it can still hurt your body.

Worry becomes a habit. You worry a little bit. Then you get used to worry. Each new thought becomes something to worry about. Your life is full of fear.

How can you break free from worry? You need a fresh way of thinking. You need to put away thoughts of worry. In their place, you need to think of God.

Take the Word of God into your mind. Let it seep into your thinking. It will drive the worry away.

Worry-Free in Seven Weeks

Why not begin something new next Sunday? I will give you a program to drive worry away. The program takes seven weeks.

You will have to learn verses from the Bible. This makes sense. Reading the Bible is the best way I know to restore clear thinking.

I will give you a new verse each week.On Sunday, learn the verse by heart. Read it over and over. Try to get it to stick in your mind.

On Monday, go over the verse again. Make sure you know it. Then be ready to repeat it when you need it. When will you need it? When a thought of worry gets into your mind. Just repeat the verse. That should help.

The next five days, do the same thing. Repeat the verse when you need it. Fight worry with the Bible.

The next Sunday I will give you a new verse to learn.

All through this time, you will be getting better. By the seventh week, the verses should be deep inside your mind. Your worry may still be there. But it won't be very strong. Your mind will be full of God's words.

If you want to, you could keep doing this program. You could find new verses. Or go back over these verses. Learn them again. If you keep filling your mind with God's Word, you can win over worry.

The Program

WEEK 1: *Learn this verse:* "I can do everything God asks me to with the help of Christ" (Philippians 4:13). This is the Bible verse for the first week. The healing starts here. Repeat this many times. Most of all, repeat it when you start to worry.

WEEK 2: *The second Sunday and all that week, use this verse:* "He will keep in perfect peace all those who trust in him." (Isaiah 26:3). Say this out loud over and over. It will seep into your thinking. It will give you peace. It will drive worry away.

WEEK 3: *This Sunday and all this week, think of this verse:* "I will not be afraid. For you are close beside me" (Psalm 23:4). This verse is full of God's power. Feel that power as you repeat the verse. Repeat this many times. Worry will not stay in a mind that is full of God. Fill your mind with God.

WEEK 4: *This week, use this verse:* "Ask, and it will be given to you; seek, and you will find; knock, and the door will be opened to you" (Luke 11:9, NIV). Jesus said this. He said that he is ready to give us the good things we need. Repeat the verse and rest in this truth.

WEEK 5: *For this week, learn this verse.* "Stay in me and obey my commands. Then you may ask for anything you like, and it will be given to you!" (John 15:7). Jesus said this, too. When he says "live," it's like moving in. We move into a new house and stay there. In the same way, we move into Jesus. His words move into us. When we ask to be free from worry, it will happen. Jesus wants that, too.

A PRAYER WHEN YOU'RE WORRIED

Dear Lord, I am worried and full of fear. I wonder what is going to happen. Could it be that my love for you is weak? Is that why I am feeling such worry?

I have told myself that there is nothing to worry about. But this does not seem to help. I know I should just rest in you. I should trust you to care for me. But I have been too nervous to do that.

Touch me, dear Lord, with your peace. Help this crazy mind of mine to rest in you. Help me to know that you are God. I don't need to fear evil. You are with me.

I pray this in Christ's name.

Amen.

WEEK 6: *On the sixth Sunday, and this whole week, repeat this verse.* "You might pray for anything. And if you believe, you will have it. It's yours!" (Mark 11:24).

WEEK 7: *For the last week of the program, learn this:* "Let God have all your worries and cares. He is always thinking about you and watching everything that concerns you" (1 Peter 5:7). God loves you. He will carry all your worries on his back. Repeat these words until they are part of you. Let your mind rest in the thought. God carries your worries. God cares for you.

If you try this for seven weeks, you will be amazed. You will change. If you were going downhill, you will go uphill. If you were upset by worry, you will be breaking free from it. If you were filled with fear, you will now be filled with trust.

CHAPTER 6

The Banker Who Changed

One Sunday, a banker came to my church. He ran a bank in New York City. He did not believe in Christ. He was the kind of person who tried to put down the faith of others.

But he saw an ad in the paper. It told the title of my next sermon. It said, "You Can Get Rid of Worry."

He thought this was crazy. Any smart person would know that you can't get rid of worry. Or so he thought. But the idea stuck in his head. It grabbed him and would not let go.

So there he was in church. He was still trying to laugh at what I said. He still thought it was crazy. But there was a need deep inside him. He was nervous. He was worried.

Because of his worry, he was not happy. Sometimes he was too nervous to work. If he didn't do his job, he would be kicked out. This made him worry even more. And worry kept him from doing his job.

As he sat there, the Lord began to talk to him. He wasn't laughing anymore. He wasn't making fun of me. He was like a patient in a doctor's office. God was the

Great Doctor. And God healed him. Right there in the pew.

The man could not believe what happened. "I can't explain it," he told me later. "The church was so full of love and faith, I could not fight it. It was like Jesus was by my side. He said, 'Come to me. I will give you rest.' I knew Jesus as a child, but I had lost him. That Sunday, he took me back."

Then he went home. And the changes stayed with him. "I was amazed at how clear my mind was," he said. "I felt a cool, calm sense of power. It was a great feeling. I hadn't felt like that in months."

He began to write down his worries. He put each one on a slip of paper. His old worries. His new worries. He wrote them all down. Then he looked them over.

He looked at all the things he had worried about. "What if this happens? What if that happens?" That's what he used to say. But now he saw that most of those things had never happened. He put all these papers into a pile.

All of a sudden, he swept up that pile of papers. Then he dropped them into a trash can. "Thank you, dear Lord," he said. "You have changed me. I am different. I feel it. I know it."

He still had some papers on his desk. These were the things that still might happen. *A few months ago, I would have been all upset about these,* he thought. *Now I know that the Lord and I can take care of them.* He was at peace.

As he told me this, I reached into my pocket. I showed him a card that I always carry with me. It says, "Lord, help me to know this. Nothing will happen today that you and I can't handle."

"That's for me," the banker said. He copied down the saying. "I'll carry it in my pocket, too," he said, "and in my thoughts."

The Lord swept worry away from this man's life. When he found the Lord, he found life. He stopped worrying and started living. Really living. He is now in charge of himself. Why? Because the Lord is in charge of him. Christ can put a new spirit in any person's heart. This new spirit is full of faith. It has no room for worry.

ALWAYS ADD UP THE BEST

A friend of mine once talked with Henry Ford. Ford, you know, was the great car maker. My friend asked him if worry was ever a problem for him.

Mr. Ford said that it used to be. But then he became "too busy to worry." He then gave my friend his surefire way to beat worry. It went something like this:

Believe in the best.

Think your best.

Study your best.

Have a goal for your best.

Don't accept any less than your best.

Try your best.

And in the long run, things will turn out for the best.

Always add up the best.

Add Up Your Blessings

There was a hymn people used to sing. It went like this. "Count your blessings. Name them one by one." The song was right on target. When you add up your blessings, your worries will get the message. They will pack up and leave.

A man called me once with a problem. He had read some of the papers we put out. He decided to call for help.

"It is all going so badly," he said. "I am worried sick."

"Maybe it's not so bad," I said. "Maybe your worry is making you see things in the wrong light."

"No, no," he said. "My whole life is washed up. Finished. It's just all gone. Nothing left but a mess of worries. Nothing else at all."

"Oh," I said. "I'm sorry to hear that your wife has left you."

"Who said she left me?" the man said. "She loves me very much. She will stay with me to the end."

"That's great," I said. "Let's do this. Let's count up what you have lost. And let's count up what you have left. Let's start with what you have left, what you still have. Then we'll get to all the things you have lost."

"Well, we won't have much to talk about," he said sadly. "I don't have anything left."

"Well, to start with," I said, "I can think of one thing. Your wife loves you. She will stay with you. But too bad your kids are taking drugs and in jail."

"My kids are not taking drugs!" the man shouted.

"They are good kids. They have never been near a jail!"

"Great!" I said. "Then that's something else you still have. Let's add that to the list. 'Children not in jail.' But it sure is tough about your house burning down. And you weren't insured, because you were too poor."

"Wait a second!" the man cried. "That's all wrong! I don't know where you heard all that, but it's not true. My house did not burn down. And I'm not poor. I've got enough money to get by."

By now he knew what I was getting at.

"I'm a fool," he said. "A big fool. I never thought of all those good things. Until you started asking me, I never knew all the blessings I had."

We began to talk about his blessings. Then we prayed with each other over the phone.

He had a few bad times after that talk. But he got over them. His mind had changed. He had gone from No to Yes. He had won over worry. At age forty-five, he stopped his worry and started his life.

The same thing could happen to you.

CHAPTER 7

I Can Change for the Better

Do things need to change in your life? Of course. All people can say yes to that. Each of us has something that needs changing. Well, there's good news. You *can* change.

There is power that you can tap into. That power is God's. As God lives and works inside of you, you will change. And you may be amazed at how big those changes can be.

Where Does the Power Come From?

A man drove out to the country to see me. His wife came with him. Both were smart people. They had good jobs. But neither of them went to church.

The man said, "Helen and I are not happy. We don't know what to do. Life has gone stale. We have come to a dead end. We need help."

He went on to talk about their problems. They just were not fresh these days. Their thinking was dull. And that hurt their work. They just did not seem to have it anymore.

"We do not want to stay this way," he added. "We want to change. You are always talking about change. That's what we want. How do we get it?"

I knew they were smart people. But I had something very simple to say to them. Tapping into God's power is not hard to do. It does not take a college degree. I was not sure that they would like that fact. It might seem too easy to them.

"You don't like the way you are," I said. "Is that right? Just how deeply do you feel that?"

"Very deeply," they both said.

"And are you telling me that you want to be changed?" I asked. "You want to be changed now?"

They both said yes.

Then I said, "There may be things in your life that go against Christ's spirit. Are you willing to put these away?"

We talked a bit about what these things might be. But they really wanted to change. They were willing to go the whole way with Christ.

We talked some more. I told them how they needed to put away their bad thoughts. Their hate. Their grudges. These had to be given to Christ. These had to be emptied from their lives. They said yes. They were willing.

"Now," I went on, "no human being can give you the power you need. No human can change your life. Only Christ can do that. Are you willing to give yourselves to Christ? Will you take him as your

Savior? Will you let him make your life new?"

Each of them prayed with me. They were simple and honest prayers. They gave themselves to Christ.

This happens all the time. People begin to sense their need to change. They really, really want to change. They begin to see that Christ can change them. They turn to him. He changes them.

The change in this couple was great. Life had new meaning for them. They had new joy. They were fresh again.

They came back to me the next spring. They were happy and full of fun. Each new sight they saw was lovely. Helen was raving, "I have never seen such a spring. The skies are blue, even more blue than before. The sun is brighter. The songs of the birds even sound sweeter."

They began to use their sharp minds to write about God. They put their new thoughts into words. That way, many others could find the power that they had found.

CHAPTER 8

A Happy Home

The home can be a great place. It can help you to be very happy. It can give you lots of love. It can make you feel very good.

Or it can be bad. It can make you sad. It can fill your life with fighting. It can make you feel awful.

Most homes are somewhere in between. All of them could change for the better. Yes, even yours. And this change can start with you.

TEN STEPS TO A CHANGED LIFE

1. Know this. The power to change your life comes through faith in Christ.
2. Give yourself and all your problems to God.
3. Let go and let God.
4. Ask God for the power to live a new life. Believe that he will give it to you.
5. Read the words of Jesus in the Bible. Learn these by heart, as many as you can.
6. Ask yourself what Jesus would do. Then try doing that.

7. Pray each day. Make it a habit. Set aside a special time.
8. Read the Bible as often as you can. Take a special look at parts that seem special to you.
9. Fill your mind with thoughts of Christ.
10. Act with love and goodwill toward other people.

You have the power to change your home. It may seem that your wife is hard to deal with. Or your husband. Or your children. Or your father or mother. But you can change things.

How? Let me give you eight steps to a happy home.

1. *Let it start with you.* Decide that you will bring a new spirit into your home. No matter what the others say, you will be a force for good.

2. *Ask yourself this.* "Am I making things better in this home? Or am I making things worse? Is my home happy because of me? Or is it sad?" Be honest in your answer.

3. *Get rid of hate and doubt.* Treat each person in the home with love. Treat them all with respect. Trust them. Care about what they say.

4. *Be a love "cell."* This is a lesson from science. A cell starts out all alone. But then it grows. It divides.

Then there are two cells. Then four. Then eight. Soon there are thousands.

Well, you can be a single cell in your home. Don't tell the others that you are doing this. Just do it. Act in love. Show love to the others. Soon you will see that love spread. It will grow through your whole home.

I knew a young man like that. At first, he did not get along with his parents. He hated all that they stood for. They were bothered by the things he did. As time went on, they drifted apart. It was all very sad.

But then this boy got to know Jesus Christ. As a result, he made up his mind to change things. He would make things better in this world. And he would start at home. He began to show love to his parents. He asked for their advice. He said nice things to them. He still had his own thoughts. But he listened to what his parents were saying. He became a sweet and friendly person.

What happened? The parents returned those feelings. They began to show love to him. The parents returned those feelings. They began to show love to him. They gave him respect. His love "cell" divided and spread through his home.

5. *Build respect for each person.* Each person should respect the others in the home. We should not try to force our ways on each other. Let each person be himself. Show each person that he or she is loved. It is great to be who you are. This is the feeling that leads to peace in the home.

6. *See the real scene.* You are not going to change your home right away. It will not be easy. There may be hate buried deep. There may be grudges that people have been holding for years. It takes time. These things can change, but slowly. Start with small changes. Then let the whole thing build up steam.

7. *Trust God to change things.* God will guide your home life — if you let him. Don't forget that he has the power. He is the one who makes things happen. So stay close to him.

The Bible says, "The Lord must build a house. If he doesn't, the builders' work is useless" (Psalm 127:1). This tells us a lot about our own homes. The homes that trust in God have the power to beat their problems. Those that don't trust in God often fail.

8. *Start praying.* You don't have to say a thing about it. Just start praying for each person in your home. Each day, morning or night, pray to God. Ask him to be with each person. Maybe there is someone else in the home who will pray with you. This will help you grow closer. People who pray with each other stay with each other.

There was a twenty-year-old girl who was going through a rough time. She was trying to find herself. But she wasn't sure who she was. She was filled with hate and anger. Most of it was against her father. But then she saw a change.

"Dad," she said one night, "you're really nice. In fact, you're a good guy. Tell me what you've been doing. What's going on?"

Her father said that he had been praying. He wanted to change himself. He wanted to be a better father, a better husband. And so he started praying each day.

He stopped for a moment. Then he said softly, "I pray for all of us in this home. But mostly I pray for you. I know we have had our problems. But I have a special place for you in my heart."

"I knew you were up to something," the daughter said. She gave him a love pat. In the next few days, the two grew closer to each other. Soon the whole family knew their secret. It was the secret of prayer. And it changed the whole home.

CHAPTER 9
Enjoy Your Job

If you want to change your life, you may have to change your job.

But there are two ways to change your job. One is to leave your job and take a new one. Some people do this. They want to get rid of all the problems of the old job. They think the new job will be just fine. But it doesn't always work like that.

You can take a new job. But you take yourself with you. You can't get away from yourself. If you had problems in your old job, you may take them with you. Maybe you had thoughts of pride. Maybe you had thoughts of hate. Maybe you had problems getting along with others. Don't think that the new job will make these go away.

But there is a second way to change jobs. That is to change yourself. You don't need to get a new job. You can stay where you are. But you will be a new person.

A man called me about his job. He said it was a dead end. There was no future in it. He was going to leave it. He would find something else.

I told him about this idea of changing yourself. I told him that the old problems might follow him to a new job. Then I talked about a man we both knew. I'll call him Mr. Smith. This man was a great success. It seemed that he won at each new thing he tried.

"What do you think Mr. Smith would do?" I asked the caller. "How would he handle the job you have now?"

The man thought for a minute. "Well," he said, "I'm sure he would make it a success. He wins all the time."

"Yes," I said, "but how would he do this? What would he do?"

"I don't know," said the caller. "I don't know what he would do."

"Well," I said, "why not think about that? Think about what Mr. Smith would do with your job. How would he make it a success? Then, when you know what he would do, you do those things."

Later the man came to me again. His thinking had changed for the better. He said, "Mr. Smith is a friendly person. He always talks to others. I am going to do that too. He is a Yes Person. He sees the good things that can happen. I am going to try that too."

The man felt a lot better about his job. And you know what? His job got better. He was doing better work. He changed his job by changing himself.

CHAPTER 10

Throw Your Crutch Away

Some people feel so bad about themselves, they use
crutches. I'm not talking about real wooden crutches.
If you have a broken leg, you need to use those. I'm
talking about "soul" crutches.

Some people think they can't deal with their
problems. Some people think they are no good. Some
people think they just can't cope.

And so, these people turn to drugs. They turn to
drink. They start eating too much. They gamble.
Maybe it's some other activity that's less risky. But it's
still a crutch. Or maybe they turn to some other person.
They think that person will solve their problems. That
person becomes a crutch.

Why do people do this? What are they looking for?
They want the power to change their lives.

That's one of the things Jesus does best. He gets rid
of crutches.

Think of the lame man lying by the pool in John
5:1-9. As the story goes, an angel came sometimes to
stir the water. The first person who got into the water
was healed. This man had been lying there for years.

All the other sick people knew him. They knew he would be there, by the pool.

But he was mixed up. He seemed to like his spot by the pool. It made him feel special. He kept saying that he could not get into the water first. But that was just an excuse. He really did not want to be healed. Then he would have to face life.

But Jesus knew his mind. He asked just the right question. "Do you really want to be healed?"

The man felt odd. Jesus saw right through him. But then he felt hope for the first time. "Yes," he said firmly. "I do want to be healed."

Jesus told him to get up. He told him to throw away his crutch. He told him to start living.

And that's what he tells us, too.

One of the most common crutches today is drinking. I met one man at a party. He had too much to drink. I asked him about it.

"Why do I do this?" he said. "I really don't like it. But I am shy. I never know what to say. Drinking helps me loosen up. It makes me more outgoing. I just couldn't stand a party like this without drinking."

I think that many drink for this reason. They are really just leaning on a crutch. You don't need booze to help you talk. You just need to talk. Think about what you know. Then talk about it. You don't need to hobble around on a crutch made of booze.

It's a shame. Some people start to trust in drinking,

and they never stop. It becomes a sickness. It defeats them. It drags them down.

Even these people can be cured. There are many groups that can help them. Many have come back from defeat. They have trusted in the power of God. And they have been able to beat their problems. God has the power to do that.

So, in the name of Jesus, throw away your crutch. Enjoy life at its best.

CHAPTER **11**

The Future Waits

You have a future! You may feel like you don't. You may believe all the bad news you have heard. Others may say it's not true. But it is. You have a future.

No matter how tough things are, you have a future. No matter how hard it is to keep going, you have a future. No matter how sad you may feel right now, you have a future.

You may be old. You still have a future. You may be sick or tired. But you still have a future. You may think that life is not fair. You may have been treated poorly. You still have a future.

Your future may be full of questions. Jesus Christ has the answers. You need to put yourself in his hands. Give him your future. Then it will be great.

Some people act as if they have no future. If they keep acting that way, they may be right. But you don't need to go that way. You can make your future real. You can make it thrilling and fun. Here's how.

Believe in your future. Think about it. Talk about it. Act upon it. Put your old ways of life away. Live a new way. And put your future in God's hands.

Each new day, wake up and say, "I have a future. With God, I have a future!" That is what God wants for you. He wants you and me to live life fully. Then he wants to take us to a future in heaven. Both here and there, we have a future. And that future looks bright. Tell yourself this each day. "With God, I have a great future!"

Highway Faith

Three people were in a car. We'll call them Bob and Mary, with their daughter, Sue. They were riding on a major highway near a big city.

The road was a bit slick. It had been raining. And there were lots of cars on the road. Some cars were stopped ahead, so Bob put on the brakes.

As he looked in the mirror, Bob saw something awful. A huge truck was sliding across the highway. It was out of control. It was headed right for their car.

Crash! The truck hit their car. The car spun around. Then the truck fell right on top of the car. Glass broke. Metal folded. Gas fumes were in the air. Then there was silence.

Mary was still alive. Her knees were up against her chest. It was hard for her to breathe. She could just barely move her hands and head. The crumpled roof was just inches above her.

Bob was alive, too. But his body was twisted. One leg was bent under him. The other leg was sticking out of the car window. It was jammed against the side of the truck.

Sue was alive, too. She was flat on her back. She could hardly move.

No one was in great pain. No bones were broken. No one was bleeding. But they could not get out. The truck covered the car. It was all around them.

How did these three react? They thanked God that they were still alive. They knew God was with them in that wrecked car. They also knew that they might still die there.

A friendly face showed up at the window. A driver was looking in. He found it hard to believe they were still alive. He told them help was on its way.

The three of them prayed. They knew that the truck's fuel was spilling out. It was joining with the gas from the car. One spark could blow up the whole thing. But they prayed.

Then the roof of the car dropped in a little bit. Then more, and more. The truck was still on top of the car. It was slowly crushing the car.

An hour went by. Two hours. A fireman showed up. He had a tube hooked up to an air supply. Then they could breathe better. And what did they do? They sang hymns. "God knows how much we can take," they told each other. And they kept singing hymns of faith.

Outside, there was now a crane. It began to lift the truck. If something slipped, the truck would crush the car. So the firemen shored up the truck with wooden beams.

Three hours after the crash, Bob, Mary, and Sue got out of their car. The doctors checked them over. They were fine. People asked them, "How could you be so calm?"

"We are in God's hands," they said. "Here in this world and in the next world."

They knew they had a future. Since they were in God's hands, they had a future.

Does your "future" happen only in this life? Is death the final borderline? No. The future goes on and on. It is not bound by time. It is not bound by your age. It is not bound by being rich or poor. It is not bound by being smart or dumb. It is not bound by being pretty or ugly. It is all in Christ's hands. If you have a future in Christ, that future is for always.

So I say it again. "You have a future!"

CHAPTER 12
Four Common Problems—and How to Beat Them

How to Cope with Hard Times

1. *Say yes.* Say yes to yourself. Think of all that God has given you. Think of all the things you can do. Tell yourself that you can cope with these hard times, too.

2. *Don't panic.* Keep cool. You don't beat hard times with your feelings. You win with your mind and your actions.

3. *Take it apart.* Look at your problem. Take it apart. Each problem has lots of smaller problems. Look at each one of these. Think about how to tackle these one at a time.

4. *Think.* Make sure your mind is in gear. Sound thinking will help you beat your problems.

5. *Why me?* Do not ask, "Why me?" Do not think

about how unfair this is. All people have hard times. Life is like that.

6. *Patience.* Be patient. Hard times don't go away right away. It takes time.

7. *Accept it.* Tell God how you feel. Tell him you don't like this problem one bit. But then listen for what he wants. Maybe he wants you to go through this problem. Maybe he wants to teach you something. Maybe he wants to build up your strength. Maybe he wants you to trust in him. Tell him that you accept this problem. Tell him that you will trust him to help you deal with it.

8. *Learn.* Each hard time can teach you something. Learn from it. Then you'll be better off next time.

9. *Bigger.* Say this each day. "God is bigger than any problem that comes my way."

10. *Let go and let God.* Do all you can do. Then put the trouble in God's hands. He will take it from there.

How to Have a Good Marriage

1. *Feelings.* Children have feelings. Adults have feelings. But as we grow, our feelings change. Children are all "Me, Me, Me." Adults learn to give to others.

Some adults keep their childish feelings all their lives. They even take these into their marriage. The first "rule" of a good marriage is this. Make sure your feelings have grown up. You will work out your troubles much better if you both act like adults.

2. *Bedrock*. Any building must be built on solid ground. It's the same with a marriage. The Bible says, "The Lord must build a house. If he doesn't, the builders' work is useless" (Psalm 127:1). A good marriage needs to be built on God. God is the bedrock that will keep you firm.

3. *Argue*. That's right. To have a good marriage, you need to argue well. Talk out your problems. Discuss the best way to solve them. And argue if you feel strongly. But make sure you are acting like an adult. Make sure your feelings don't get in the way. And don't forget this. It does not matter *who* is right. You are both trying to decide *what* is right.

4. *Best*. Bring out the best in your husband or wife. He or she has great things inside. Bring those out. Give of yourself to help the other. This is the basis of a truly loving marriage.

5. *Be nice*. This is so simple. But sometimes we forget it. Be nice to your husband or wife. Do nice things. Don't let anger make you nasty. Give each other respect.

6. *Both.* Both members share a marriage. Both need to work at it. Both share in its joys. Both need to give to each other. This means that neither one should lord it over the other.

7. *Change.* You will both need to change. As the marriage goes on, you will both grow. You need to sense the changes in each other. You need to change yourself in order to keep things right. A good marriage is always changing — for the better.

8. *Team.* Live, play, and work as a team. Each partner brings something to make the marriage great. Do things with each other as often as you can. Care about what the other is doing. Decide things with each other.

9. *Night.* Pray with each other before you go to sleep. Pray about your problems. Pray about things you have to decide. The couple that prays with each other will grow with each other. They will stay with each other and win with each other.

10. *Fun.* Have fun with each other. Do all the loving things you can think of. Make this a game, a fun game. If each tries to make the other happy, the marriage will be happy.

How to Solve a Problem

1. *Seeds.* All problems can be solved. Each problem has

the seeds of its own solving. If you look deeply into the problem, you can find how to fix it.

2. *Calm.* Stay calm. If you are uptight, your mind will not work right. But if there is no stress, it will.

3. *Take it Apart.* Your problem is made up of many parts. Divide your problem into its parts.

4. *Paper.* Put the parts of the problem down on paper. Maybe just the first letter for each part. As long as you know what you're dealing with. Then look at the papers. See which parts of the problem you can start to solve. When you see this clearly, you will be able to think clearly.

5. *Force.* Never try to force an answer to a problem. Keep your mind relaxed. Make sure you are seeing straight. If you try to force an answer, it may not work. It may be what you want, rather than what is right.

6. *Pray.* Pray about the problem. Pray again. Pray some more. God will give you the wisdom you need. Just keep praying. God's wisdom will help you solve the problem.

7. *Advice.* Sometimes we need help. From God, and from others. So get good advice. Ask a pastor or

Christian teacher for help. You need to hear what God is saying. A person like this could help you.

8. *I just know it.* Do you ever have those feelings? You know, a flash in your head. A sudden thought. You say, "This is it! This is the answer! I just know it!" It may be a little crazy, but you have this feeling. Well, those feelings can be good. God sometimes gives us those flashes of insight. Don't give up your careful thinking. Keep looking at the problem to find the solution. But try out that sudden thought, too. That just might be the answer you need.

9. *Float.* Let the problem float around in your mind. Don't feel bad about it. Don't feel rushed. Relax. No deadline. No pressure. Let it float. Your mind will play with the problem. It may even come up with an answer.

10. *New.* Your mind is always coming up with new things. Trust this process. Let it happen. Keep thinking about how to solve the problem. Keep praying. Keep saying yes. God will guide you to an answer.

How to Turn Failing to Success

1. *Passing.* Failure is not here to stay. It is a passing thing. It is a short setback in a good, long life. You will learn from it. You will grow. You will put it behind you. And then you will be passing, not failing.

2. *Wrong.* Failure is the wrong way to do something. So look at the bright side. Failure tells us how not to do something. That gives us a better chance to know how it should be done.

3. *Learn.* Learn from your failures. Learn from your success. Keep your mind active. Take in the lessons of life.

4. *Never.* Never accept failure. Failure will not be a way of life for you. It may be here now. But it will not last. Soon you will move on. You will win over this failure.

5. *Think.* That great genius, Thomas Edison, had a sign on his wall. It said, "There is a better way to do it. Find it." How do you find it? Keep praying. And keep thinking.

6. *Work.* I never said it would be easy. Success is hard work. But it's good work. Good, solid work will open the door of success for you. You will enjoy both the work and its results.

7. *Goal.* Winning people have goals. Not fuzzy dreams. Clear, sharp goals. You don't get somewhere unless you know where you are going. What do you want to do? Where do you want to go? How are you going to get there? Make this a matter of prayer.

8. *Right.* Make sure your goal is a right one. Nothing

that is wrong will ever turn out right. Make sure God is guiding you to your goal.

9. *Ask.* Ask God to guide you. He will direct your life. This is the only way to true success. That is doing what God wants.

10. *Way.* The sure way to success is the way of love. This means caring for others. This means praying for others. This means giving to others.

WORD LIST

a 261	answer 13	bedrock 2	brakes 1	cars 3
able 4	answered 4	been 14	brave 4	cases 1
about 58	answers 3	before 4	break 3	cell 4
above 1	any 14	began 8	breaking 1	cells 1
accept 4	anymore 2	begin 4	breathe 2	chain 1
across 2	anything 4	behind 1	bright 2	chance 2
act 7	apart 5	being 6	brighter 1	chances 1
acted 1	are 71	believe 10	bring 4	change 38
acting 2	area 1	bent 1	brings 1	changed 11
actions 1	aren't 1	beside 1	broke 1	changes 5
active 1	argue 3	besides 1	broken 2	changing 4
activity 1	army 1	best 18	brother 2	chapter 1
actors 2	around 6	better 20	brought 1	charge 2
ad 1	as 38	between 1	brown 1	cheating 1
add 5	aside 1	Bible 14	build 7	check 2
added 4	ask 17	big 14	builders 2	checked 1
admit 4	asked 15	bigger 5	building 1	chest 1
admits 1	asking 2	bill 1	built 2	Chevalier 1
adult 1	asks 3	birds 1	burger 1	child 6
adults 4	at 44	bit 6	burgers 2	childish 1
advice 13	ate 1	bits 1	buried 3	children 5
afraid 26	attack 1	blank 1	burn 1	Christ 15
after 5	attitude 1	bleeding 1	burning 1	Christ's 3
again 14	aware 1	blessings 5	busy 2	Christian 1
against 6	away 25	blob 2	but 93	church 4
age 3	awful 2	blow 2	buy 1	city 9
ago 2	back 10	blows 3	by 25	civil 1
ahead 2	bad 10	blue 2	call 7	clear 3
air 2	badly 1	boat 3	called 5	clearly 2
alive 6	bank 1	Bob 5	caller 2	climb 1
all 69	banker 3	body 3	calm 6	close 3
almost 2	barely 1	bones 1	came 10	closer 2
alone 1	basis 1	book 2	can 95	coast 1
along 3	be 118	booth 1	can't 13	college 1
also 3	beams 1	booze 2	car 15	come 11
always 19	beat 8	borderline 1	card 1	comes 3
am 17	beaten 1	boss 9	care 7	coming 1
amazed 3	beats 1	both 18	career 1	commands 1
amen 1	beauty 3	bother 1	careful 2	common 2
an 17	became 4	bothered 1	cares 2	complain 1
and 143	because 7	bound 5	caring 1	concerns 1
angel 1	become 5	bowl 1	Carlyle 1	control 1
anger 2	becomes 4	boy 1	carries 1	cool 4
another 3	bed 1	brain 1	carry 5	cope 3

copied *1*
copy *2*
could *20*
couldn't *1*
count *3*
counter *2*
country *1*
counts *1*
couple *2*
course *3*
cover *1*
covered *1*
cow *1*
cowboy *2*
cows *6*
crane *1*
crash *2*
crazy *4*
cried *2*
crippled *1*
crowd *2*
crumpled *1*
crush *1*
crushing *1*
crutch *7*
crutches *5*
cured *1*
cut *1*
cutting *1*
dad *1*
daring *1*
dark *1*
daughter *2*
David *1*
day *15*
days *3*
dead *2*
deadline *1*
deal *12*
dealing *2*
dealt *1*
dear *3*
death *2*
decide *5*
decided *2*
deep *5*
deeply *4*
defeat *1*
defeats *1*
degree *1*
dent *1*
desire *2*

desk *3*
details *2*
Detroit *1*
did *20*
didn't *1*
die *1*
different *1*
diner *1*
direct *1*
discuss *1*
divide *2*
divided *1*
divides *1*
dizzy *1*
do *83*
doctor *6*
doctor's *1*
doctors *1*
does *9*
doesn't *7*
doing *10*
don't *44*
done *2*
door *2*
doubt *1*
down *17*
downhill *1*
drags *1*
drain *1*
dreams *1*
drifted *1*
drifts *2*
drink *3*
drinking *4*
drive *4*
driver *1*
drives *1*
dropped *2*
drove *1*
drugs *3*
dull *2*
dumb *1*
during *1*
each *57*
easy *5*
eating *2*
Edison *1*
effort *1*
eight *3*
eleven *1*
else *6*
emptied *1*

empty *1*
end *5*
enjoy *5*
enough *1*
Ephesians *1*
even *12*
ever *6*
every *2*
everything *3*
evil *2*
example *1*
excite *1*
excites *1*
excuse *2*
explain *2*
extra *1*
eyes *2*
face *7*
facing *3*
fact *7*
facts *5*
fade *1*
faded *1*
fading *1*
fail *8*
failed *2*
failing *6*
failure *13*
failures *1*
fair *2*
faith *10*
family *1*
famous *2*
far *2*
fast *1*
father *4*
fear *41*
feared *1*
fearful *3*
fears *14*
feel *17*
feeling *5*
feelings *14*
feet *1*
fell *1*
fellow *1*
felt *9*
fence *1*
ferry *2*
few *4*
fight *3*
fighting *1*

fights *1*
figured *1*
fill *4*
filled *3*
filling *1*
final *1*
find *16*
fine *2*
finger *2*
finished *1*
fire *2*
fireman *1*
firemen *1*
firm *3*
firmly *1*
first *15*
fit *1*
five *4*
fix *2*
flair *1*
flash *1*
flashes *1*
flat *1*
float *3*
flow *1*
fog *3*
foggy *1*
fold *1*
folded *1*
follow *1*
fool *2*
for *82*
force *5*
Ford *3*
forget *5*
forty-five *1*
found *5*
four *3*
France *1*
Fred *8*
Fred's *1*
free *6*
freed *1*
freeze *1*
freezing *1*
French *1*
fresh *3*
friend *10*
friendly *5*
friends *1*
friendships *2*
from *39*

front *3*
frowned *1*
fuel *1*
full *16*
fully *2*
fumes *1*
fun *25*
future *31*
fuzzy *1*
gamble *1*
game *2*
gas *2*
gave *7*
gear *1*
genius *2*
get *38*
gets *5*
getting *4*
gift *2*
girl *1*
give *24*
given *5*
gives *4*
giving *2*
glad *3*
glass *1*
glory *1*
glows *1*
go *27*
goal *4*
goals *2*
God *62*
God's *16*
goes *6*
going *17*
gone *3*
good *32*
goodwill *1*
got *11*
grabbed *1*
grace *2*
great *33*
greatest *2*
grew *1*
ground *1*
group *1*
groups *1*
grow *7*
grown *1*
grows *1*
grudges *2*
guess *2*

guide *4*	him *62*	its *9*	lesson *4*	makes *5*
guiding *1*	himself *4*	Jackson *3*	lessons *3*	making *4*
guy *1*	his *74*	jail *3*	let *27*	man *37*
guys *1*	hit *3*	jammed *1*	let's *8*	man's *3*
habit *2*	hobble *1*	Jeremiah *1*	lets *1*	many *14*
had *48*	holding *1*	Jersey *1*	letter *1*	Mark *1*
hadn't *1*	holy *1*	Jesus *15*	level *1*	marriage *12*
hall *1*	home *22*	job *21*	licked *1*	Mary *3*
hand *4*	homes *3*	jobs *3*	lie *1*	matter *7*
handle *5*	honest *4*	John *3*	life *58*	Maurice *4*
handled *1*	honor *1*	joining *1*	life's *2*	may *29*
hands *8*	hooked *1*	jokes *1*	lift *1*	maybe *17*
hang *1*	hope *1*	Joshua *1*	light *1*	me *74*
happen *12*	hoping *1*	joy *11*	lights *2*	mean *6*
happened *9*	horn *1*	joys *1*	like *37*	meaning *1*
happens *3*	hot *2*	jumble *1*	line *1*	means *6*
happy *13*	hour *1*	just *39*	lined *1*	meet *1*
hard *20*	hours *2*	keep *23*	lines *1*	meeting *2*
harder *2*	house *5*	keeps *3*	list *1*	melts *1*
hardly *1*	how *56*	kept *3*	listen *2*	members *1*
has *19*	huge *1*	kick *2*	listened *1*	men *1*
hate *6*	human *2*	kicked *1*	lit *1*	merely *1*
hated *1*	hunched *1*	kids *4*	little *8*	mess *1*
have *90*	hurt *2*	kill *1*	live *7*	message *1*
having *4*	hurts *1*	kind *9*	lives *5*	met *2*
he *278*	husband *4*	knees *1*	living *4*	metal *1*
head *3*	husbands *2*	knew *21*	lonely *1*	middle *1*
head-on *1*	hymn *1*	knock *2*	long *7*	might *11*
headed *2*	hymns *2*	know *38*	look *19*	mighty *1*
heads *1*	I *200*	know-how *1*	looked *6*	mind *31*
healed *5*	I'd *1*	known *1*	looking *6*	minds *5*
healing *1*	I'll *3*	knows *2*	looks *3*	mine *4*
hear *4*	I'm *19*	lame *1*	loosen *1*	minute *1*
heard *5*	I've *1*	land *1*	Lord *15*	minutes *2*
heart *4*	ice *1*	large *1*	lose *7*	mirror *1*
heaven *1*	idea *3*	last *2*	losses *1*	miss *5*
height *1*	if *49*	later *3*	lost *8*	mist *1*
Helen *2*	in *147*	laugh *1*	lot *9*	mistakes *1*
hello *1*	inches *1*	laughed *1*	lots *4*	mixed *1*
help *33*	ink *1*	laughing *2*	loud *1*	moment *2*
helped *1*	inner *1*	lead *1*	love *32*	Monday *1*
helps *3*	inside *7*	leader *1*	loved *1*	money *1*
Henry *2*	insight *1*	leaders *2*	lovely *1*	months *2*
her *18*	instead *2*	leads *3*	loves *4*	mood *1*
here *13*	insured *1*	leaning *1*	loving *2*	moon *1*
here's *2*	into *26*	learn *21*	luke *1*	more *11*
Hereford *1*	involved *1*	learned *3*	lying *2*	morning *3*
Herefords *1*	is *158*	least *2*	made *12*	most *10*
herself *2*	Isaiah *1*	leave *4*	major *1*	mostly *1*
hidden *1*	isn't *1*	left *6*	make *27*	mother *3*
hide-and-seek *1*	it *226*	leg *3*	make-believe *1*	mother's *1*
highway *3*	it's *15*	less *2*	maker *1*	mountains *1*

move 7	or 24	poor 3	report 1	seep 2
moved 2	order 3	poorest 1	respect 7	sees 3
moving 1	ordered 1	poorly 1	rest 6	sell 5
Mr. 6	other 45	power 20	restore 1	sense 8
much 10	others 20	pray 21	result 1	sent 1
must 8	our 10	prayed 5	results 1	sermon 1
my 40	out 34	prayer 3	return 1	set 1
myself 3	outgoing 1	prayers 1	returned 2	setback 1
name 7	outside 2	praying 8	rich 1	sets 1
nasty 1	over 24	prays 1	rid 10	seven 4
near 2	own 7	pressure 1	riding 1	seventh 1
neatly 1	owned 1	pretty 7	right 29	shake 2
need 43	pack 1	pride 1	risky 1	shaking 1
needed 2	page 1	printer's 1	river 1	shame 1
needs 6	paid 2	problem 43	road 2	share 2
neither 2	pain 1	problems 33	romance 1	sharp 3
nerves 1	panic 2	process 1	roof 2	she 37
nervous 3	paper 6	product 1	room 1	sheet 1
never 25	papers 5	program 5	rough 2	sheets 1
new 45	parents 6	promise 2	rule 1	shines 1
news 3	part 5	proves 1	run 2	shored 1
newsman 1	partner 2	Psalm 6	runs 1	short 1
next 9	parts 7	pull 1	rushed 1	should 19
nice 5	party 2	put 20	sad 8	shoulder 3
night 9	passing 3	question 2	sadly 1	shouldn't 1
nine 1	pastor 1	questions 2	safe 1	shouted 1
ninety-five 1	pat 1	quiet 2	said 87	show 9
no 45	patience 1	quit 2	salesman 3	showed 3
nodded 1	patient 2	quite 1	salesmen 3	showing 1
normal 2	peace 5	quitting 1	same 7	shy 4
Norman 4	people 51	rabbit 1	sang 4	shyness 1
not 81	percent 2	races 1	sat 1	sick 4
nothing 7	perfect 3	rail 1	Savior 1	sickness 1
now 22	perk 1	rain 1	saw 8	side 4
number 4	person 38	raining 1	say 26	sight 1
obey 1	person's 1	ran 1	saying 11	sign 2
odd 1	Peter 1	ranch 1	says 12	silence 1
odds 1	pew 1	rather 1	scare 1	silly 1
of 208	Philippians 2	raving 1	scared 3	simple 6
off 3	phone 5	reach 1	scares 2	since 2
office 5	pieces 1	reached 1	scene 1	sing 3
often 7	pile 3	react 4	science 1	singer 2
oh 3	piles 1	read 5	second 4	singing 1
OK 2	place 7	reading 2	secret 6	single 1
old 13	places 1	ready 3	see 18	sir 2
older 2	plan 2	real 6	seeds 2	sitting 2
on 58	planning 1	really 19	seeing 2	six 1
once 9	play 6	reason 3	seek 1	sixth 1
one 56	please 1	rejoice 1	seem 9	size 2
only 10	pocket 2	relax 2	seemed 7	skies 1
open 1	poked 1	relaxed 1	seems 1	sky 1
opened 1	pool 3	repeat 11	seen 1	slave 1

sleep *1*	stage *3*	taken *2*	through *13*	upon *1*
slick *1*	stale *1*	takes *4*	throw *3*	upset *3*
sliding *1*	stand *4*	taking *2*	time *25*	uptight *1*
slip *1*	stands *1*	talk *17*	times *12*	us *18*
slipped *1*	start *23*	talked *5*	Timothy *1*	use *6*
slowly *2*	started *9*	talking *6*	tired *2*	used *6*
small *4*	starts *2*	talks *3*	title *1*	useless *2*
smaller *1*	stay *15*	tall *4*	to *376*	verse *18*
smart *5*	stayed *2*	tap *1*	today *3*	verses *4*
smile *1*	stays *1*	tapping *1*	told *25*	very *19*
smiled *2*	steam *1*	target *1*	tonight *2*	visiting *1*
smiling *2*	steel *1*	teach *4*	too *23*	voice *1*
Smith *4*	step *1*	teacher *1*	took *1*	wait *5*
snow *2*	steps *5*	team *4*	top *3*	waiting *1*
so *37*	stick *1*	teased *1*	touch *1*	waits *1*
soft *1*	sticking *1*	tell *17*	touched *1*	wake *1*
softly *2*	still *20*	telling *4*	tough *7*	walks *1*
sold *1*	stir *1*	tells *3*	toward *1*	wall *2*
solid *2*	Stonewall *2*	ten *2*	town *1*	want *20*
solution *1*	stood *4*	tend *1*	track *1*	wanted *5*
solve *7*	stop *5*	tends *1*	train *1*	wants *12*
solved *1*	stopped *6*	tense *1*	trash *1*	war *1*
solving *2*	stops *1*	than *9*	treasure *2*	was *125*
some *30*	stores *1*	thank *1*	treat *2*	washed *1*
someone *6*	storms *3*	thanked *1*	treated *2*	wasn't *3*
something *29*	story *3*	that *159*	tried *5*	watch *1*
sometimes *6*	straight *2*	that's *21*	tries *1*	watching *1*
somewhere *2*	strange *3*	the *409*	trouble *2*	water *3*
son *1*	strength *1*	their *34*	troubles *1*	waved *1*
song *1*	stress *1*	them *68*	truck *9*	way *40*
songs *1*	strong *3*	themselves *2*	truck's *1*	ways *4*
soon *4*	stronger *1*	then *64*	true *3*	we *49*
sorry *1*	strongly *1*	there *63*	truly *2*	we'll *3*
sort *1*	stuck *1*	there's *3*	trust *11*	weak *1*
soul *1*	study *2*	these *24*	trusted *1*	week *16*
sound *2*	stutter *1*	they *117*	truth *1*	weeks *4*
sounded *1*	success *15*	thing *12*	try *15*	well *16*
soup *1*	successes *1*	things *53*	trying *7*	went *19*
South *1*	such *3*	think *43*	tube *1*	were *37*
southern *1*	sudden *3*	thinker *4*	turn *10*	weren't *1*
spark *1*	Sue *3*	thinking *15*	turned *1*	west *1*
sparkle *1*	sun *1*	thinks *2*	twelve *1*	what *63*
special *10*	Sunday *8*	this *139*	twenty-year-old *1*	what's *4*
speech *1*	supply *1*	Thomas *2*	twisted *1*	when *28*
spilling *1*	sure *18*	Thoreau *1*	two *9*	where *6*
spirit *8*	surefire *1*	those *19*	ugly *1*	which *1*
spite *3*	sweet *1*	thought *15*	under *4*	who *25*
spoke *4*	sweeter *1*	thoughts *11*	unfair *1*	whole *9*
spot *2*	swept *2*	thousands *1*	unless *1*	why *18*
spread *3*	table *1*	three *8*	until *4*	wife *6*
spring *2*	tackle *1*	thrill *2*	up *51*	will *111*
spun *1*	take *27*	thrilling *5*	uphill *1*	willing *4*

win *11*	wives *2*	working *1*	wrecked *1*	you'll *1*
wind *5*	woman *3*	works *2*	write *3*	you're *4*
window *2*	won *3*	world *10*	writer *1*	you've *1*
winning *1*	won't *9*	worried *5*	written *1*	young *7*
wins *3*	wonder *2*	worries *9*	wrong *5*	younger *1*
winter *1*	wooden *2*	worry *37*	wrote *1*	your *138*
wisdom *3*	word *2*	worry-free *1*	years *5*	yours *3*
wise *4*	words *7*	worrying *1*	yes *22*	yourself *25*
wiser *1*	work *21*	worse *1*	York *2*	yourselves *1*
with *100*	worked *3*	would *34*	you *417*	
without *2*	worker *1*	wreck *1*	you'd *1*